SR/A LT

OP '87

DRAWINGS FOR THE THEATRE

DRAWINGS FOR THE THEATRE

By

ROBERT EDMOND JONES

THEATRE ARTS BOOKS

NEW YORK

PUBLISHER'S NOTE

For the second edition of this important milestone in the history of American scene design the publishers have taken one liberty with the original. In it PLATE THIRTY-FIVE, a photograph, rather than a drawing of the set of *Anna Christie* was reproduced too small to be effective. In its place we have put a drawing of *Lute Song,* 1946, discussed in detail by Donald Oenslager in his 1969 introduction. The Introduction by Arthur Hopkins in the first edition has been deleted.

ACKNOWLEDGEMENT

This record of ten years' work in the theatre has been made and published through the interest of Edith J. R. Isaacs. That the reproductions give in such large measure the quality of my original drawings is due to the cooperation of Mr. Francis Bruguière, who made the photographs. and of Mr. Harry A. Groesbeck, Jr., who watched over the engraving of the plates.

Published by THEATRE ARTS BOOKS
333 Sixth Avenue / New York, New York 10014

Printed in the United States of America

TABLE OF CONTENTS

INTRODUCTION TO THE SECOND EDITION

BETWEEN 1915 and 1940 there was a resonant explosion of activity in our theatre in the work of the younger generation of playwrights, directors, designers and actors. Idealistic groups asserted themselves with infectious enthusiasm. New alignments with the professional theatre were established. The growth of this new movement marked a stimulating and exciting time in the American Theatre.

The designers most responsible for the new visual directions of this theatre were the triumvirate, Lee Simonson, Norman Bel Geddes and Robert Edmond Jones. Together they established Stage Design as an Art in the Theatre and gave the visual theatre impetus and recognition throughout our country. They were chiefly responsible for gathering the stage designers into a union organization. While these three designers were close friends, each had his own creative goals and concept of design not only of scenery for the conventional theatre but also of tomorrow's theatre architecture which might house their new style of design.

Robert Edmond Jones burst into public consciousness on the night of January 27, 1915 with his setting and costumes for *The Man Who Married A Dumb Wife* by Anatole France. Within ten years, when *Drawings for the Theatre* was first published, the old artless style was passé and the revolution effected by Jones, Simonson and Bel Geddes was triumphant, magnificently so, as the designs of Robert Edmond Jones in this volume attest.

I first came to New York the year before that, in 1924, and I was privileged to work with Bobby Jones, as everyone affectionately called him in those days, for one season as an assistant—better to say as an apprentice. Afterward, all through the years, he and I remained close friends.

It is significant that Mr. Jones was of New England stock, born in the small town of Milton in New Hampshire and in a house which had been occupied by his family for generations. This long, rambling structure included a roadside tavern built in 1810 and his bedroom was the former "ladies' retiring room" on the second floor of the tavern. The oldest part of the house inspired his design for the Cabot Homestead for *Desire Under the Elms* by Eugene O'Neill.

The Jones' farm was a working farm. His father read Dickens propped up on one plow handle as he followed his horses down the long furrows of the rich valley! Mrs. Jones was a musician who had attended the Boston Conservatory of Music. She taught young Robert to play the violin and encouraged his growing interest in drawing. When he was 19, young Jones broke from New Hampshire tradition and went to Harvard College in Massachusetts, graduating in 1910.

At Harvard he concerned himself with the Fine Arts, developed his drawing and painting under the distinguished artist and teacher, Denman Ross. He occupied himself with little or no activity in the theatre. However, on occasion he did indulge himself by going into Boston to B. F. Keith's Theatre where he was enamored with the magical, dazzling and theatrical allure of such divas and sirens as Valesca Seurat and gorgeous Gertrude Hoffman.

After two years as an instructor at Harvard, he found his way from New England to Europe where he discovered the force of the New Movement in the theatre and surrendered himself to its irresistible appeal. He was in Florence the year Gordon Craig founded his Theatre School in his Arena Goldoni but, strange to say, even though armed with a letter of introduction to Craig and while he admired

Craig's spatial innovations enormously, he was not enrolled in the school. He found wonderment in Claudel's *L'Annonce faite à Marie*, presented in the revolutionary theatre of Appia and Dalcroze in the latter's school at Hellerau outside Dresden. Jacques Copeau had just installed his aspiring company in his new Théâtre du Vieux Colombier in Paris. He moved to Berlin and became enthusiastically involved with Max Reinhardt and his two principal designers, Emil Orlik and Ernst Stern, in the Deutsches Theater. He was working on a production of *The Merchant of Venice* and also an unproduced play for Budapest when the First World War broke out and Jones came back to New York.

After his "wanderjahr" in Europe, Jones returned to attack our theatre's stronghold of false realism. As an artist, fortified with his vision of "the new stagecraft," he soon opened new doors and illuminated new paths. As a craftsman, he discovered new ways and means of employing canvas and scene paint and light. His unorthodox designs were unembroidered with realism. They suggested mood by understatement and expressed the essence of his concept of a scene.

Lee Simonson perceptively relates his art to his New England background: "Robert Edmond Jones, as an artist and as a person, was a unique combination of craftsman, romantic, mystic and Puritan. His feeling for the materials he worked with and his skill in manipulating them were akin to those of our colonial craftsmen who gave a clear and enduring beauty to their silverware, chairs and chests, porticos and staircases, their steeples and weather vanes, frigates and figureheads. His profession was less a calling than a call, like the 'call' that led some of his New England forebears to the pulpit. The soul to be saved was the theatre's. His aim, throughout his career, was not only to recover its pristine purity and splendor by his own efforts but also to inspire all workers in the theatre—authors, actors, directors, as well as fellow designers—to enlist in his crusade. . . . Jones' work was not simply a profession, in the accepted sense, but a continual dedication. For he possessed both the vision of an artist and the imagination of a militant visionary."

Two of his Harvard classmates and admirers deeply interested in the new visual theatre arranged an exhibition of stage designs in a vacant Fifth Avenue store. In this exhibition Jones' drawings for the theatre attracted the attention of another young theatre enthusiast—an impresario and stage director, Arthur Hopkins, who at once engaged Jones to design his production of Anatole France's *The Man Who Married A Dumb Wife* with the English director, Harley Granville-Barker. This production was a tremendous success and marked the beginning of a collaboration between Jones and Hopkins for many years to come, evidenced by Hopkins' introduction to the first edition of this book.

The simplicity and style of Jones' design for this play (Plate One) with its medieval background was indeed a turning point in America for the visual theatre. It was a complete break with the realistic traditions of the contemporary theatre epitomized in the photographic realism of the productions of David Belasco. Jones established once and for all the importance of the artist in the theatre.

It has been said that a man who works with his hands is a workman; a man who works with his hands and his head is a craftsman; and when that man also works with his heart, he is an artist. From his first production, Robert Edmond Jones combined these three roles with triple felicity.

To understand Robert Edmond Jones' scope as an artist turn to his 1920 designs for the Jones-Hopkins production of *Richard III,* with John Barrymore playing Richard (Plates Six, Seven, Eight and Nine). Jones always considered himself the servant of the play. He envisioned the entire play set within a massive, stone courtyard inspired by the Tower of London, the set to occupy the entire stage and rise to its full height. These weighty walls were always present as a brooding background. For changes of scene an arras, a cage for a prison or a wall were rolled out to the center of the stage. For the final scene (Plate Nine) the black silhouette of a gibbet against a blood red sky dramatized visually the closing action of the drama. With this production Jones achieved simplification, a multi-scene basic setting that "worked" for the whole play, and an impression of soaring visual unity among all the scenes.

The same imaginative approach was evident in the production which Jones and Nijinsky as choreographer and dancer evolved for the Richard Strauss tone poem *Til Eulenspiegel* (Plate Three). Diaghilev presented the ballet at the Metropolitan Opera House in 1916 when his troupe could not perform in Europe during World War I. Here is a "witches' brew" of flying buttresses, medieval towers and turrets, all out of scale and intended to convey an impression of the wild visions and pranks of the young Til.

For Mr. Jones the scene designer was always a man of many minds. According to the dictates of the drama, he thought in terms of realism or surrealism, of impressionism or expressionism, or symbolism. He trained his eye on the conventions of all the arts, past and present. Yet while he was a man of many minds, every production was invariably finished with the patina of his own special polish.

What constituted a good scene in the eyes of Mr. Jones? "A good scene is not a picture. It is something seen, but it is something conveyed as well; a feeling, an evocation. A setting is not just a beautiful thing, a collection of beautiful things. It is a presence, a mood, a symphonic accompaniment to the drama, a great warm wind fanning the drama to flame. It echoes, it enhances, it animates. It is an expectancy, a foreboding, a tension. It says nothing, but it gives everything."

To animate his stage scene with his special sense of theatre, Jones relied enormously on the power and the versatility of stage lighting. For the Jones-Hopkins production of *Hamlet* with John Barrymore in 1922 he designed a spacious Great Hall whose towering walls rising high enclosed a flight of stairs that led from the width of the forestage back to a dominating Romanesque arch (See Plate Twenty-three). There were no scene changes, only changes of light and two front curtains. (Plates Twenty and Twenty-one.) He played light like a chiaroscuro wash over some scenes; at other times an exploring spotlight revealed the inner content of a dramatic situation. Scene by scene his use of arbitrary light activated the forward movement of the drama.

One critic referred to this permanent setting as "a cathedral of the mind." Another unwittingly said that "Ophelia was buried in the parlor"! The entire production was conceived in terms of fluid light playing on fluid action. Light with Jones was always a marvelously sensitive medium of expression, so sympathetic that "the livingness of light" for him was almost a sixth sense. For his "new theatre" he sought "the shadowless light" by way of "colored light and colored shadow leading gradually to a halcyon light that is colorless and without shadow." He thought of lighting as a craft and had no rules for its use. "Our real problem in the theatre is to know where to put the light and where to take it away."

Another facet of Mr. Jones' talent was his sense of craftsmanship, his almost oriental feeling for fabrics and material and their special finish. *Lute Song* was perhaps Mr. Jones' last large-scale, significant assignment. Starring Mary Martin, it was directed by John Houseman in 1946. (Plate Thirty-five.) It was a musical play for the modern theatre based on an ancient Chinese drama. There was a great variety of scenes and all were freely changed in view of the audience. The scenes and properties might have been done actually by the designer himself in the tradition of an Eastern craftsman, so careful was their execution.

His working drawings for *Lute Song* were impeccable models of lucid definition and explanation. His blueprint for the Rain Curtain specifies that it be "made of 4-inch strips of shiny satin in several shades of gray brushed with black and silver—should be doubled and stitched at both sides but not lined."

With Jones, the craftsman never took over where the artist left off because with him the artist never left off; the felicity and completeness of his drawings were an inspiration to the craftsmen concerned with executing the production. This capacity for translating the actual into the exaggerated terms of the theatrical was most characteristic of Jones' work in the theatre.

Throughout his career Mr. Jones was ever aggressive in his concern for experimentation. He was always exploring old ways of achieving new directions for the theatre of today and tomorrow. An experiment in fusing light and space was his project for Shelley's drama *The Cenci,* which he designed very early in his career. (See Plates Twenty-nine to Thirty-three.) Jones visualized this production as taking place on the central raised stage of a sports arena; the stage from below and overhead to be harshly lighted with the white light of the boxing ring. (Plate Twenty-nine.) He hoped that the characters of this stark tragedy should appear externalized as though seen through the eye of an x-ray—in costumes of blacks and whites with intrusions of violent red.

For scenery he used actors carrying properties. They appeared stark and theatrical within the darkness of the surrounding audience.

Another one of Mr. Jones' adventurous works was the Jones-Hopkins production of *Macbeth* with Lionel Barrymore in 1921. In their interpretation of the play they sought "to release the radium of Shakespeare from the vessel of tradition." Hopkins wrote in the program: "So to us the tragedy of *Macbeth* is not the series of incidental murders and deaths, but it is that strong people can be picked up by forces they do not understand, are helpless to combat, and by which they are dashed to utter destruction.

"This we believe to be the immortal phase of *Macbeth,* since it is a tragic condition of all time.

"As to settings, we have left behind all compromise with realism. They are just the barest beginnings of things. We believe they will be of great beauty.

"So this is our dream. It may prove wonderful or terrible, but it at least represents our feelings for the play. No other consideration has interfered."

The stage was enclosed in blackness. High above hung three silver masks (Plates Twelve and Fourteen)—the forces of destiny looking down upon and controlling the course of the characters of Shakespeare's drama. Identical masks were worn by the witches (Plate Twelve). The indications of scenery which Jones employed were indeed "just the barest beginnings of things." At that time Jones was deeply concerned with psychoanalysis and his brief suggestions of these scenes for *Macbeth* resembled personified abstractions—indications of place seen through the mind's eye of the characters of the play. In the Letter Scene (Plate Thirteen), Lady Macbeth found her way, as in her own dream world, between twisted and tormented frames.

For the Banquet Scene (Plate Fourteen) there were the masks overhead, the tottering throne of Macbeth before a splotch of red against a white wall. Shattering illumination played over the unstable banquet table. Referring to this *Macbeth,* the critic Stark Young declared, ". . . there was a lustre, a high intention; and, both outwardly and at the core, there was a poetry, elusive and moving, such as we have had nowhere else in our theatre." Lacking perceptive direction this avant garde production was an artistic failure. I suspect today it might have the success it deserved forty-eight years ago.

In the early twenties Robert Edmond Jones, Eugene O'Neill and Kenneth MacGowan formed an alliance, Experimental Theatre Inc., and for three years operated the Provincetown and the Greenwich Village Theatres in Lower Manhattan with the intention of presenting in their way the finest theatre of the past and the present in these two intimate playhouses. They gathered together a young and dedicated acting company of ten, augmented by "guest players," and also technical associates. I was one of those acolytes assisting Mr. Jones. Possibly twenty-five productions were presented, some indeed highly experimental. All were imbued with vitality, vision and idealism. These Off-Broadway productions exerted a strong influence on the professional Broadway Theatre.

Plate Thirty-three is a design for Eugene O'Neill's dramatic arrangement of Coleridge's poem *The Ancient Mariner.* The settings were projected on the Provincetown stage's cyclorama. The performers wore masks. Mr. Jones designed and also directed this production in which he was exploring the subtle relationship of actor and scenery. He believed: "*The essence of a stage setting* lies in its incompleteness. A setting is planned with great care to enhance the characteristic qualities of actors and their performances, and it does not really exist without them. It is arranged around the particular happenings of the play.

They are its focus, its central point. It contains the promise of a completion, a promise which the actor later fulfills. It is charged with a sense of expectancy. It waits for the actor, and not until the actor has made his entrance does it become an organic whole."

A scenic approach in a totally different direction was Robert Edmond Jones' design for Congreve's comedy, *Love for Love,* at the Greenwich Village Theatre (Plate Twenty-eight). The setting is a stylization of the formal English Restoration stage. The "make believe" setting was fashioned of mirrors, of cheap, showy, metallic fabrics with tinsel chandeliers. The costumes also were highly theatrical. Here Mr. Jones was likewise the director and his direction vividly reflected the polish and exaggerated style and wit which we associate with the artificiality of the Restoration Theatre.

The design for Eugene O'Neill's *Desire Under the Elms* (Plate Twenty-six) was for another production of Experimental Theatre Inc. It reveals his selective capacity as an artist for distilling in a stage setting the essence of a realistic background. The two elm trees framing either side of the stage serve as sentinels, observers of all the strange, immoral conflicts of those who inhabit this remote New England farm. The unnatural foliage of the sheltering trees seems to take on the very life of the Cabot household. The stern façade of this house, which can be removed to reveal four interior scenes, exudes the tragic mood and atmosphere of O'Neill's somber play.

These three productions indicate the variety of theatre this group offered their subscribers. It was an exciting venture. For lack of funds it could not survive.

Mr. Jones wrote as an artist with perceptive sensitivity about his own world of the theatre. In addition to *Drawings for the Theatre,* he published a second book, *The Dramatic Imagination,* a series of essays which remains one of the most illuminating books on our theatre. A third volume, *The Theatre of Robert Edmond Jones,* edited by Ralph Pendleton, was published by the Wesleyan University Press. This contains essays by artists and writers on Jones' contribution to the theatre, and it includes reproductions of many of his sketches, a record of his productions, and a chronology of his life.

At one time Mr. Jones sought to establish a synthesis between the theatre and motion pictures. He explored many possibilities in his desire to create this new form of theatre art—in a new form of theatre building. He set down his prophetic ideas which younger designers, notably Ralph Alswang, have explored and which the choreographer Alwin Nikolais has recently extended with his Sound and Vision Theatre. Abstract sculptors and painters (not of the theatre) like Rauschenberg, collaborating with illuminating engineers and composers of electronic sound, have created "happenings," adventurous theatre forms unrelated to our theatre of today, but directly out of what Jones in 1924 called "a presentation of light, color, moving form and sound —an abstract evocation—a dream that is living with 'life beyond life.' "

In 1934 Jones was invited to Hollywood where, stimulated in an alien field, he devised and designed for Pioneer Pictures the first colored motion pictures that were made. "Color Designs by Robert Edmond Jones" were made for *La Cucaracha,* followed by *Becky Sharp* directed by Rouben Mamoulian. These films in Technicolor were to become milestones in the development of cinematic art.

Although he continued his work as a theatre artist for twenty-six years after the publication of *Designs for the Theatre,* the drawings which he selected in 1925 for this book prefigure in a remarkable way the total career of Robert Edmond Jones and summarize the breadth of his talent and the depth of his artistry. While these drawings are in black and white, I think they give the quality of his sketches. So often he used luminous blacks and grey washes, or pen and ink with occasional flashes of brilliant red or an indicative accent of color. Metallics he delighted in too for their sheer theatricality.

Two productions Mr. Jones designed later should be mentioned because they were such dramatic extensions of his early innovations. The first was his design for the street scene (Act III) of Gounod's opera *Faust,* done for the American Opera Company in 1928. With three simple pieces of scenery he established and dramatized all the aura of a medieval town, and of the Faust story. The second was Mr. Jones' conception for Stravinsky's *Oedipus Rex,* presented first in the United States in 1931 at the Metropolitan Opera House by the League of Composers. The vast stage was engulfed in black. There was no scenery. The singers were placed unseen with the orchestra in the pit. The chorus in dark, hooded robes sat on bleachers stretched across the dark stage. The characters of this musical drama, as Jones had envisioned it, were played by enormous marionettes, twelve feet high brilliantly executed from his designs by his friend, Remo Bufano. They suggested masked, archaic figures of the ancient Greek world. Disembodied, they floated through the air in stark light high above the chorus, with slow, hierarchic gestures and in eerie, stylized rhythms. It was the essence of drama, past and present.

Robert Edmond Jones' health began to fail in the late 1940s. He continued with his designing and writing until he retreated from the ephemeral world of the theatre and returned to the Jones Farm in New Hampshire. On Thanksgiving Day, 1954 he died in the same canopied bed he had known all his life.

His dreams for our American theatre, however, live on. His influence on the younger generation survives and will continue to survive through his inspired writings and evocative drawings for the theatre. John Mason Brown, the late distinguished drama critic, had a deep appreciation of Mr. Jones' talent. He wrote that: "His settings were not reproductions of reality. They were extensions of it. They had exaltation in them, too. Although the mood and meaning of a play lived in them, they lived a life of their own. This is why Bobby's sketches have out-lasted the productions for which they were made and will continue to do so. The dream that was his walks in them, as summoning as ever, and the more welcome and needed in today's almost dreamless theatre, as reminders of what the theatre can be."

DONALD OENSLAGER

THE SOUL OF THE ARTIST
From an Old Thibetan Painting

FOREWORD

OVER my desk as I write there hangs an old painting brought from Thibet, It is called "The Soul of the Artist." Out of the bottom of the picture rise the topmost peaks of the tallest mountains of our world, the world of everyday objects and images. High above this world hovers a mythical horse, the Thibetan Pegasus, bearing on his back the figure of the Artist. Horse and rider are bound to one another by heavy chains. With one hand the Artist brandishes aloft his staff of power; in the other he holds his own heart, torn from his body, bleeding and burning. He is hurried away through the abyss of the sky by a strange shadowy being clad in the lion-skin of courage. His spiritual attributes hover around him—birds and curious heraldic beasts and fantastic monsters—beautiful, excessive, terrible. At the very top of the picture three gods rest in their heaven—a heaven now somewhat worn and rubbed and seeming therefore even more mysterious and unknowable. And all around and about these vivid esoteric symbols—Pegasus, the Artist, the gods, the extravagant birds and camels and dragons—the old painter-visionary has set a pattern of myriads of tiny flames. A glowing air, a region of fire wherein the Soul of the Artist must forever move and have its being.

I reproduce the picture here because this ideal artist-figure, soaring high above our earth in its flight toward an unknown heaven—powerful, tortured, free—seems to me always a symbol of the ideal Actor, and this background of fire a symbol of the ideal stage-setting. The scene-designer is forced to work and think in a hundred different ways—now as an architect, now as a house-painter, now as an electrician, now as a dressmaker, now as a sculptor, now as a jeweler. He must make idols and palaces and necklaces and frescoes and caparisons. As he works he may be all too well aware of the outward limitations of the play he is to decorate and the actors he is to clothe But in his mind's eye he must see the high original intention of the dramatist, and follow it; and the actors who out of the range of their own knowledge and their wisdom are to recreate that vision on the stage must seem to him what the artist seemed to the old Thibetan painter, pure Spirit, ascending The designer's sole ambition must be to affirm and ennoble the art of these mystical Protagonists. And he may rest content only when we say, as the curtain rises on the work of his hands: *It is evident that this play we are about to see is no common play. It is evident that these men and women who will appear before us are no common mummers. These are Actors, Seers, Sayers. Let us honor them. For by their inspiration they intimate immortality.*

ROBERT EDMOND JONES.

New York, July, 1925.

[24]

TO THE ACTOR

THE MAN WHO MARRIED A DUMB WIFE

PLATE TWO

CALIBAN

A Shakespeare Interlude combining scenes from
The Merchant of Venice, Romeo and Juliet, The Winter's Tale

TIL EULENSPIEGEL: Before the Cathedral

PLATE FOUR
THE JEST, Act III
The Pillar

PLATE FIVE

La Cena Delle Beffe, Act II

Ginevra's Chamber

KING RICHARD III, Act I, Scene II

The Wooing of Lady Anne

KING RICHARD III

Gloster's Soliloquy (interpolated from *King Henry VI*)

KING RICHARD III, Act I, Scene IV

Clarence in Prison

KING RICHARD III, Act V, Scene IV

A Gibbet

THE BIRTHDAY OF THE INFANTA, Scene I
The Courtyard of the Palace

The Birthday of the Infanta, Scene II

The Hall of the Mirrors

MACBETH, Act I, Scene I

The Three Witches

MACBETH, Act I, Scene V

The Letter Scene

MACBETH, Act III, Scene IV

The Banquet Scene

PELLÉAS ET MÉLISANDE, Act IV, Scene III

The Fountain

SWORDS

A Castle in Calabria

HIMMLISCHE UND IRDISCHE LIEBE (LAUNZI), Act V
The Tower Room

BEYOND

Fireside

HAMLET, Act I, Scene II

The Court

HAMLET, Act I, Scene III

A Curtain

HAMLET, Act III, Scene III

A Curtain

HAMLET, Act III, Scene IV

The Queen's Closet

HAMLET, Act V, Scene I

The Burial of Ophelia

THE SAINT

The Portico of a Seminary at Las Flores, New Mexico

The Star, Scene II

The Astrologer on the Bridge

PLATE TWENTY-SIX

DESIRE UNDER THE ELMS

The Cabot Homestead

The Cenci, Act I, Scene III

The Banquet

THE CENCI, Act IV, Scene IV

The Arrest of Beatrice

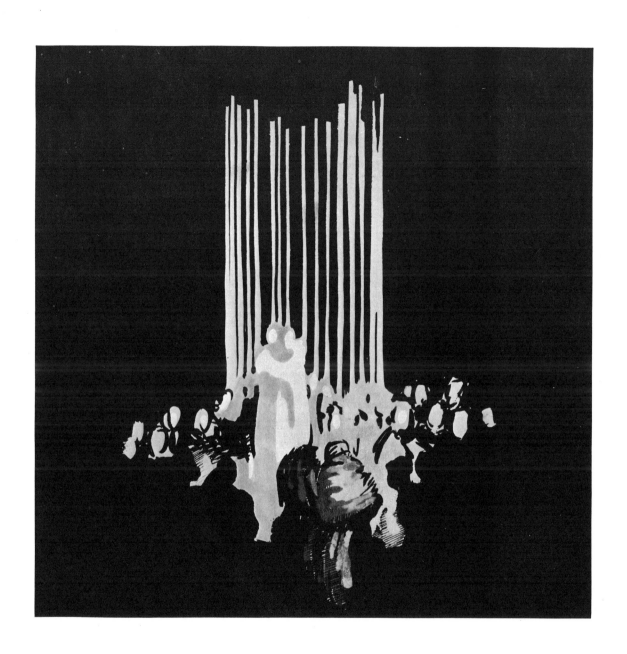

The Cenci, Act V, Scene IV

The Final Scene

AT THE GATEWAY

LUTE SONG

The Blue Pavilion in the Palace of Prince Nieou

As THE *actors of our stages get their masks and their costumes, robes of state or rags, so a Soul is allotted its own fortunes, and not at haphazard but always under a Reason: it adapts itself to the Fortunes assigned to it, ranges itself rightly to the drama, to the whole principle of the piece. Then it speaks out its own business, exhibiting at the same time all that a soul can express of its own quality, as a singer in a song. . . . But these actors, souls, hold a peculiar dignity. They act in a vaster place than any stage. The Author has made them masters of all this world.*

—PLOTINUS.

TH/   N/037JMK

Jones

N/037JMK

Jones